D1029200

Pole Bending

Matthew Broyles

rosen
central™

The Rosen Publishing Group, Inc., New York

Dedicated to Danny Dutton, cowboy poet.

Published in 2006 by The Rosen Publishing Group, Inc.
29 East 21st Street, New York, NY 10010

Library of Congress Cataloging-in-Publication Data

Broyles, Matthew.
Pole bending/Matthew Broyles.—1st ed.
    p. cm.—(The world of rodeo)
Includes bibliographical references and index.
ISBN 1-4042-0547-0 (library binding)
1. Pole bending. I. Title. II. Series.
GV1834.45.P34B76 2006
791.84—dc22

2005017550

Manufactured in Malaysia

On the cover: Lacy Wilson turns the final pole at a pole-bending event at the New Mexico High School Rodeo at the Otero County Fairgrounds in Alamogordo, New Mexico, on May 1, 2004.

Contents

Introduction

On any given Saturday, horses and riders throughout the United States gather together to compete in a rodeo event whose origins go back thousands of years: pole bending. Though each horse and rider team rides for less than a minute, the speed and energy that are required for this unique event are breathtaking to behold. So, too, are the precision and form that are showcased in pole bending, as years of training and practice are brought together for a few seconds of high-intensity horsemanship.

Though not as well-known as the more rambunctious and dangerous rodeo events, such as bull riding or bronco busting, pole bending has been around for far longer. It also doesn't raise the same concerns over animal rights that other rodeo events do, since the whole idea of the event is that a horse and rider must work together in perfect harmony and mutual understanding in order to succeed.

Pole bending is also distinct from most other rodeo events in its diversity of participants. Generally, there is a good mix of male and female riders at pole-bending competitions. Pole bending is also an event that children and teenagers, as well as adults, can compete in, making it a truly inclusive sport.

Angie Bennett of Angleton, Texas, weaves through the poles in an early round of the International Finals Youth Rodeo, held at the Oklahoma Expo Center in Shawnee, Oklahoma, in July 2002. The rodeo drew more than 1,000 competitors, including international participants.

THE ORIGINS OF POLE BENDING

CHAPTER 1

The origins of pole bending are difficult to trace. Most rodeo events, such as calf roping and bronco busting, developed from practical ranch work. Cattle had to be herded and wild horses "broken," or tamed for riding. Pole bending, on the other hand, developed out of the practice of ancient techniques of military horsemanship. It evolved further as it was integrated into the growing sport of rodeo. Pole bending as an equestrian sport has three distinct sources: dressage, gymkhana, and rodeo.

DRESSAGE

In the fourth century BC, the first book on training a horse for riding was written by a Greek historian and sportsman named Xenophon (circa 431–350 BC). Until that time, horses in Europe had been trained primarily for pulling chariots rather than carrying individual riders on their backs. But cavalries of mounted horsemen travel faster and are easier to maneuver than fleets of chariots. The wheels and axles of chariots tended to break, and chariots were difficult to control on rough terrain. Over the next several hundred years, and particularly starting in the sixteenth century AD, the idea of horsemanship as an art developed gradually across Europe, eventually becoming known as dressage, a French term that means "training."

In the nineteenth century, interest in dressage grew rapidly, and before long, it became popular among wealthy equestrians. Masking dressage took a lot of time and the core and maintenance of horses required a lot of money, two commodities that less well-off riders did not possess. By 1912, dressage was an Olympic sport, with the first Olympic dressage events held in Sweden. Riders in Europe, Asia, and the Middle East all developed their own unique forms of dressage. One of the most important dressage academies was the Spanish Riding School in Vienna, Austria, which became known around the world for the amazing feats of its student riders and their Lipizzaner horses.

The idea of dressage is to develop a graceful, responsive horse that interacts perfectly with its rider, who in turn should also be well trained to respond to the horse. The exercises that are featured in dressage competitions are meant to develop the horse's natural athletic abilities and willingness to perform, thereby making it a better riding horse. These exercises include walks, trots, canters, sidewise canters, zigzag canters,

The fourth-century-BC Greek soldier and historian Xenophon is pictured above on horseback. His work *On the Art of Horsemanship* is the oldest surviving text on horseback riding, and the first work known to emphasize the horse's emotional well-being.

passages (slow-motion trots), piaffes (trotting in place), and pirouettes. A panel of judges scores these exercises based on skill and grace. Horse and rider must be in almost perfect sync to execute these movements gracefully.

Successful competition is not always the primary goal of dressage. Sometimes the training of the horse and the development of a rider's skills are ends in themselves. The theory is that horses and riders who have been properly trained will be able

Greek Horses in Asia

The origins of equestrian games in Greece and India may not be unrelated. In 326 BC, Alexander the Great conquered the lands of modern-day India and Afghanistan. Alexander's armies pioneered military practices such as tent pegging, and similar horse-and-lance techniques were used against the elephant-mounted armies of Alexander's Indian enemies. Greek mounted warriors would spear the weak spots in the elephants' toes with lances in order to cripple them and stall their advance.

to perform equestrian activities—whether for work, sport, or pleasure—better than those who do not have any experience with the discipline of dressage. Nevertheless, dressage is an important and popular equestrian sport, with competitions televised around the world.

GYMKHANA

From the late seventeenth through the early twentieth centuries, during the Raj—the period of British rule of the Indian subcontinent (which today includes the formerly British-controlled India, Pakistan, and Bangladesh, as well as Sri Lanka, Nepal, and Bhutan)—British soldiers used horses both for transportation and military purposes. Horsemanship was an ancient tradition in Asia, where the Chinese had been mastering the art of riding since at least 1000 BC.

Combining these Eastern equestrian traditions with those from Europe, the British cavalry began holding games on Sunday afternoons designed to train both horses and riders for combat. These games became known as gymkhana, perhaps derived from the Hindi word *gedkhana*, which literally means "ball court," but may have more generally referred to sports contests and athletic skills. Gymkhana refers specifically to competitive games on horseback.

One of the purposes of gymkhana was to simulate combat situations. Classic events include ring spearing and tent pegging, both of which were useful military

A Sikh rider prepares to take part in a tent-pegging demonstration in Anandpur Sahib, in the Punjab region of India. Tent pegging is one of several martial arts on display—including archery and sword fencing—during the annual Hola Mohalla festival. This festival is held over three days and commemorates the military battles of Sikhs over their enemies.

training exercises. In ring spearing, a horse and rider would gallop full speed toward a ring, which the rider would try to lance. Tent pegging is a gymkhana event that involves using a lance to remove tent pegs from the ground. This tactic was used to collapse the tents of the enemy and cause chaos in their camp. Similarly, pole bending is thought to have developed from exercises that simulated situations in which cavalry had to ride quickly through forests, weaving in and out of trees in pursuit of enemies.

Upon returning to Britain, the soldiers brought gymkhana back with them. Over the years, new events were added, and gymkhana meets had many local variations, including games that were inspired by Native American equestrian practices. While

Pole Bending

initially popular with all kinds of riders, gymkhana competitions eventually became associated with younger riders. Perhaps the smaller ponies used by children were more suited to the games than larger, less maneuverable steeds ridden by adults. In gymkhanas held in Europe and the United States, pole bending remains a favorite sport of young riders, although a small community of older riders enjoys it also.

It is unclear whether modern pole bending derives more from the Eastern gymkhana or Western dressage, but elements of the two traditions have been merged in the pole-bending events featured in the rodeo competitions held throughout North America today.

RODEO

From the time of the Spanish conquistadores of the sixteenth century, horsemanship was an important part of life in the American West. In Spain, only the wealthy were allowed to ride horses. But with the large numbers of cattle that needed to be grazed, corralled, and herded across the vast landscape of the New World, it became necessary to train servants in horseback riding. These working-class riders were called vaqueros, or "cattle tenders." The English term was "cowboy." Many of those who traveled west during the Gold Rush of the 1840s but failed to make their fortune instead learned cowboy skills from the vaqueros and worked on cattle ranches.

At the end of a long day of ranch work, cowboys would often gather in the stockyards and compete to see who was the best rider or roper. Crowds would often gather to watch these informal competitions, sometimes placing bets on who would win. As the twentieth century approached, cowboy work became more scarce, thanks to increased private landholding, the creation of parkland, and the introduction of roads and cattle trucks, and the use of cattle chutes for branding and vaccinating (rather than roping and dragging individual cattle). Riders began to hold competitions less for their own amusement and more to keep their cowboy heritage alive.

Before long, local citizens began lining up to buy tickets to these events, which became known as rodeos. The name comes from the Spanish word *rodear,*

A cowboy breaks a wild horse in a corral at the LS Ranch in Texas in 1907. Breaking a horse basically means riding it until it becomes used to a rider and saddle and no longer bucks. This practice of taming wild horses for ranch work, also known as bronco busting, evolved into the rodeo sports of saddle bronc riding and bareback riding.

which means "to surround," as in a cattle roundup. Soon, talented cowboys started to make more money from their rodeo winnings than from what little cowboy work remained, and rodeo as a profession and a way of life was born.

Showmen like William Cody (better known as Buffalo Bill) began to recognize moneymaking potential in these then-informal competitions. Buffalo Bill, a gold prospector, Union scout, Pony Express rider, buffalo hunter, author, actor, and entertainment entrepreneur, organized the first Wild West shows. These outdoor, circuslike spectacles introduced audiences to the history and mythology of Western frontier life, including real buffalo hunts and reenactments of Indian attacks, Pony Express rides, and Custer's Last Stand. Buffalo Bill's shows also

Buffalo Bill's Wild West shows featured expert horsemanship, trick roping, and sharpshooting. The popularity of its Western-themed entertainment and thrilling riding feats helped lead to the development of rodeo. The Wild West shows also presented historical scenes, including reenactments of battles between Native Americans and white settlers. Buffalo Bill employed Native Americans for these scenes, one of which is depicted above in this 1899 advertisement.

introduced events such as trick riding and fancy roping. Many of the showy equestrian events of these Wild West shows eventually found their way into rodeo and are now competitive events today.

By the early 1900s, rodeo had become big business. At the turn of the century, stories of cowboys and the Wild West were pouring out of magazine and book printing presses in the East and even in Europe and elsewhere around the world. The popular mythology of the American cowboy was being developed and growing on the spot, and the whole world was captivated. The romantic figure of the cowboy was only enhanced by the introduction of movies in the first decade of the twentieth century. The popularity of movies, which often featured Western stories, drove rodeo attendance and profitability even higher.

THE PRCA

To keep rules and judging consistent for each of the many rodeo competitions that were springing up across the West, the Professional Rodeo Cowboys Association, or PRCA, was formed in 1936 as the Cowboys Turtle Association. In 1945, the group's name changed to the Rodeo Cowboys Association, and finally to the PRCA in 1975. As the popularity of rodeos grew, promoters were driven to add more and more events to their shows, including timed events that demonstrated riding skills. As with its gymkhana-influenced counterpart, barrel racing, pole-bending riders are often female. This is because in most major rodeo circuits and associations (including the PRCA), women do not often compete with men in events like steer wrestling, calf roping, bronco busting, and bull riding. However, members of the Women's Professional Rodeo Association (WPRA) can compete in barrel racing in PRCA-sanctioned rodeos. Members of the sister organization, the Professional Women's Rodeo Association (PWRA) can compete in all-women's rodeos, which include such events as bull and bronc riding and calf roping.

While many of North America's most prestigious rodeos are sanctioned by the PRCA, premier pole-bending events are sanctioned by the American Quarter Horse Association, or AQHA, which holds the pole-bending World Championship, open to both men and women. Founded in 1940, the AQHA is the official record-keeping organization of quarter horses and quarter horse competitions in the United States. Quarter horses, the most popular breed of horse in pole bending, are compact and muscular saddle horses known for their endurance and high speed over short distances.

Pole bending is practiced in a few countries outside the United States, mostly in Europe. Italy, Denmark, and France include pole bending as part of dressage competitions. Australia has an active pole-bending association as well.

POLE-BENDING CHAMPIONS

CHAPTER 2

Those who compete in pole bending are part of a surprisingly small and tight-knit community. Unlike many rodeo sports, pole bending is not well known by people who aren't riders themselves. As a result, its champions tend to be humble and unassuming. They compete for the challenge and the pure enjoyment of the experience rather than for fame.

More often than not, champion pole benders credit their horses with victory rather than their own skills. Lonnie Willen credits his horse more than himself for his winning run in the 2004 Amateur World Championship. "He did it, it wasn't me! He was doing it on his own," said Willen, as quoted in Christine Hamilton's article "Amateur Pole Bending Finals" for the AQHA Web site. "It's not because I rode him, he's just easy to train. He likes the turns."

Even among young riders who could be expected to be brash and boastful, there's a tendency to give the horse the honors. Seventeen-year-old Kelli Johnson, 2004 youth World Champion, said of her winning run in the 2004 youth World Championship, as quoted on the AQHA Web site: "After I turned my second end pole, I knew we had a great run going. It was so quick, and I was always told that's [my horse's] money pole."

Pole-bending riders are also very diplomatic. When asked to name favorites from among past pole-bending champions, the common answer is, "Oh, I don't have any favorites." When pressed further, this initial statement is often followed by lists of their friends who have recently competed.

Champion pole-bending horses, however, do become famous and sought-after, though in a manner very different from that of celebrities hounded for autographs. Breeding quarter horses is big business for owners. Winning horses fetch higher prices since it is hoped that their excellent racing genes will be passed on to their offspring, who may be money-earning champions of the future. Rene Dan Jet is one of North America's most famous pole-bending horses. He won four World Championships and has sired many foals as a result. Many of his offspring have become champions themselves. Renes Jet Charge, Kitadan, and Charlies Jet Chick are among the most prominent and successful Rene Dan Jet foals.

Lonnie Willen rides his horse, Dinkys Honor Bound, during the 2004 AQHA World Championship Amateur pole-bending finals. This winning ride of 19.9 seconds earned them the world championship trophy.

Most pole-bending riders also compete in other rodeo events, since award money in pole bending is not as great as in events such as barrel racing. Award money varies and comes from the entry fees each rider puts up to compete. Because of the relatively small pool of competitors, pole bending is one of the easiest sports for new riders to start competing in. Winning, of course, is another matter.

INTERVIEW WITH KATHY BALLINGER

The world champion of the American Quarter Horse Association's pole-bending competition for two years running has been Kathy Ballinger of Lonsdale, Arkansas (the Senior finals in 2002 and the Amateur finals in 2003), riding Song of Badlandsskip.

Pole Bending

Kathy Ballinger *(standing)* poses with her horse Song of Badlandsskip (also affectionately called Old Slow Fred) after they won the Senior pole bending finals at the 2004 AQHA World Championships. Their winning time was 19.473 seconds.

Before she purchased Song of Badlandsskip, his nickname, ironically, was Old Slow Fred. They've been riding together for ten years and have developed a strong bond. Ballinger spoke to the author via telephone from her ranch in Lonsdale, Arkansas, in April 2005.

When asked how long she had been competing in pole bending, Ballinger replied, "I've been competing for ten years, starting when I was thirty, but I've been riding since my teens. When I got [Old Slow] Fred, we started showing, and we learned together. My daughter, Crystal, is now competing. She's thirteen." Old Slow Fred earned his name while Ballinger was looking him over and considering purchasing him. Everyone told her he couldn't run fast, but together Fred and Ballinger proved the nay-sayers wrong.

Surprisingly, Ballinger finds that interest in pole bending is not as high in her home state of Arkansas as it is in northern states. "I sure wish more folks down here would take a look at pole bending," she said. "It's a great sport, but it just hasn't caught on as much here." When asked why that might be, she answered, "I really don't know. Maybe they just haven't seen it yet. If they saw it, I think they'd like it."

Ballinger has her favorites when it comes to pole-bending riders. "There's a guy from Canada, Edwin Cameron, who's real good. Also Darrell Logan, he rode a horse called Lassie Lender to the senior championships a few years ago." But a horse

The American quarter horse (like the one pictured above) is descended from Arab, Turk, and Barb breeds that were brought to the New World and bred together. The result was a compact, heavily muscled horse that could run a short distance over a straightaway extremely fast. For this reason, the breed became a popular racing horse in colonial America. Quarter horses moved west with the pioneers and began to be used on ranches. Over time, quarter horses began to be trained for many different kinds of competitions, including show jumping, barrel racing, calf roping, and pole bending.

and rider don't have to win to get her respect. "There's a horse named Redneck Jet, the rider's name is Trent Tobin. He has trouble at the World Championships, and I don't know why, because he's a good horse everywhere else. Good horse, rotten luck."

Asked for her advice to young pole-bending riders, Ballinger keeps it simple. "Start out slow. Stop when the horse hits the poles. He needs to know he's not supposed to hit them. Just keep on doing that, and you'll have a great horse."

POLE-BENDING BASICS

CHAPTER 3

Though pole bending is a relatively simple, straight-forward event, it requires an enormous amount of skill on the part of horse and rider, many hours of practice, and investment in a fair amount of equipment. Any successful pole-bending career will begin, first and foremost, with the horse.

THE HORSE

Ken Smith of Sunrise West Quarter Horses in Clarkston, Washington, spoke to the author via telephone from his ranch in Clarkston, Washington, in April 2005. Asked to describe the essence of the event, he said, "Pole bending is precision dressage at speed. It is a dance with your horse. Things happen rapidly at this event. Barrel racing is slow motion compared to pole bending." Because the hallmarks of pole bending are the display of both speed and precision in maneuvering around tight turns, a winning horse must be flexible above all else.

Trainers use the term flexion to describe the way a horse's flexibility can be measured. According to Smith, "Look to see if the horse passes the poles with an arc in his body to match the pole being passed—a slight right arc for a pole on the right, and a slight left arc for a pole on the left." To be capable of demonstrating the proper amount of flexion for each pass around the poles, the horse must be in good shape. The horse must also be symmetrically straight, which most horses aren't. Just as humans are naturally either right-handed or left-handed, most

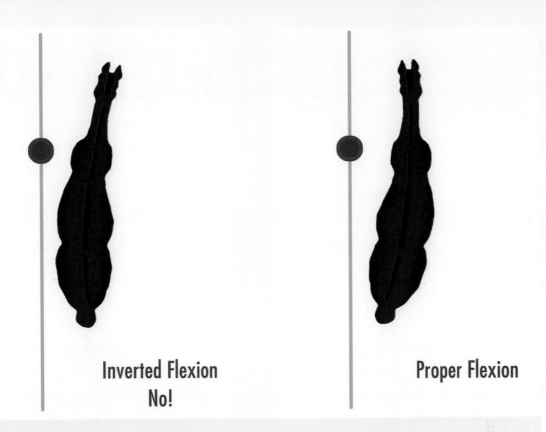

**Inverted Flexion
No!**

Proper Flexion

For maximum efficiency of movement, a horse should always be flexed in the direction it is turning. This is known as proper flexion. Inverted flexion is when a horse is flexed away from the direction in which it wishes to turn. The diagram above shows both inverted and proper flexion as a horse approaches a pole (the dark dot). Sometimes improper flexion is caused by the rider who uses the outside rein (the one farthest from the pole) to keep the horse safely away from the pole in order to avoid knocking it over. This reining pulls the horse out of its proper turning motion. The rider should instead use his or her inner leg and inner rein to direct the horse into the turn and away from the pole.

horses are "flexed" to one side or the other. And just as the majority of humans are right-handed, most horses are flexed to the right.

In his book, *Nineteen Second Pole Bending*, trainer Wayne Sandberg explains, "Most authorities agree that the majority of horses are naturally asymmetrical to the right. The muscles of the right of the horse are flexed while those of the left are extended." This means that horses will show better flexion on right turns than on left turns, with the result that they cannot run the entire course smoothly and fluidly.

Although most horses are asymmetrical to the left or right, there are some that are born with equal flexion on both sides. These are called naturals, and they often win more competitions than those born asymmetrical. Horses don't have to be born symmetrical, however; they can be made to be symmetrical. Getting the horse symmetrically straight is the goal of pole-bending trainers who have developed many exercises to make horses equally flexed on the left and right sides. Therefore, the naturals will not necessarily win every competition.

Flexion is not the only quality to look for in a pole-bending horse. Footfall is an important element as well. Ken Smith told the author, "Look to see if the horse makes it past each pole in two strides. Three strides out of the turns, then two strides between the other poles." Ponies and smaller horses may take extra strides to cross those same distances, but in general, the fewer footfalls per turn, the better.

Quarter horses are generally preferred in pole bending, but any type of horse may be used. The most important requirement for a pole-bending horse is a good temperament, including patience, focus, and obedience, all of which come with careful training. A horse with large, clear eyes is thought to be more trainable. The horse should be able to back, sidepass, and calmly change from a lope to a trot to a run, and vice versa. Above all, a horse should be willing; it should want to be ridden and worked. Older horses are more seasoned and calmer, and therefore softer. New riders should consider buying or learning on horses that are fourteen years or older.

THE RIDER

The horse is only one component of a winning pole-bending team. The rider is every bit as important. A good rider knows when to direct the horse and when to stay out of the horse's way and let its own instincts and physical prowess take over. As Smith says, "I think we are just beginning to see the effects of applying horsemanship principles from 2,000 years ago. Most pole benders, including world champions, pull their horses to direct them. Great horsemen 'send' their horses,

Kati Phillips of Douglas, Wyoming, crosses through the poles during a pole-bending event at the National High School Finals Rodeo, held in Gillette, Wyoming, in July 2005. The National High School Rodeo Association (NHSRA) is an independent student athletic association that offers competitors the opportunity to earn educational scholarships and grants. The top four NHSRA contestants in each event in each state qualify for the National High School Finals Rodeo. More than 1,500 contestants from each of the more than forty state and provincial associations compete for national titles, awards, and scholarships.

with more of a pushing method." Many modern horsemen are beginning to take this approach, drawing out and gently guiding the horses' natural skills and instincts rather than commanding them through brute force.

Generally, there are four aids that enable a rider to guide a horse: legs, hands, weight, and voice. A horse can be directed and guided by the pressure of the rider's legs on its sides, the use of reins held in the rider's hand, the shifting of the rider's weight to either side of the horse, and the use of vocal commands (to stop, slow down, speed up, back up, move forward, etc.).

Pole-bending riders start early, most of them as children, learning to guide the horse with the four aids. Though riders do not always own the horses they

The saddle pictured above is designed specifically for speed events, such as pole bending. The rigging (the straps that run from the saddle to underneath the horse) is set low and away from the rider's leg to avoid entanglements. This also allows the rider's legs to lie right against the horse's sides, increasing the pressure and control the rider can exert. The saddle has a wide base that increases its stability and decreases slippage. The fender, the leather piece that hangs between the saddle and the stirrup, swivels at the rider's knee and moves in harmony with the rider's lower leg, while allowing the upper leg to remain still. The saddle is also designed to sit forward on the horse, placing the rider's legs just behind the horse's soldiers, the ideal position for a pole bender.

ride, horse-and-rider teams have been known to stay together for many years, participating in many competitions and building their reputations together.

Unlike many other rodeo events, especially those sanctioned by the Professional Rodeo Cowboys Association (PRCA), the leading rodeo association in the United States, men and women often compete in pole bending together, depending on the organization that sanctions the race. Women have always been involved in rodeo. Several popular events, such as barrel racing, breakaway calf roping, and goat tying, are generally women-only in most rodeos. In addition, women can compete in bull riding, bronc riding, and roping events in PWRA-sanctioned rodeos.

TACK

In rodeo events, a rider's gear is called tack. Tack includes most of the equipment that will be put on the horse, from its mouth down to its tail. The most noticeable and well-known piece of tack is the saddle.

What is now called the Western saddle was derived from the Spanish saddle of the fifteenth century. The general design of the saddles in use today had been developed by the mid-nineteenth century. The most noticeable addition to the Spanish saddle by the vaqueros and cowboys was the saddle horn, a knobby piece of leather. A cowboy would tie one end of a rope to the saddle horn before lassoing a cow, thereby keeping the rope anchored to the saddle and horse rather than the cowboy's hand. This design innovation saved cowboys' thumbs, which used to get yanked off by cattle pulling hard at the other end of the rope. The type of saddle used in pole bending varies, but two of the most common types are the Texas and Santa Fe saddles. These saddles were both designed specifically for cowboy work before being adopted by pole benders.

The saddle horn also provides a handle of sorts to grab and steady oneself with, especially when turning the last pole at each end of the course. This differs from Western dressage, in which the rider is not allowed to grab the saddle horn for balance, something many inexperienced riders will do. Instead, dressage riders must maintain balance and control with their legs, while keeping their feet in the stirrups.

Pole Bending

The stirrups pictured above feature a 30-degree bend that mimics the natural curve of the foot, improving comfort and balance for the rider. The twist also makes it harder to fall out of and easier to get back into the stirrups.

The use of stirrups can be traced back to Asia in the second century BC, and few modern saddles come without them. They enable riders to stay in the saddle more easily and give commands to their horses through the pressure of their legs. As mentioned previously, the riders' legs are one of the four aids that are typically used to direct the horse in pole bending. But the stirrups can also be used in conjunction with another of the four aids—weight. Riders can shift their weight in the saddle, putting themselves in a good position for the horse to maneuver around poles. Shifting their weight, applying pressure with their legs, and using the reins also indicate to the horse in what direction it should go.

In a pole-bending competition, the rider must be careful when using the reins. If the horse has been trained well, it will need very little guidance to go smoothly through the poles. According to Wayne Sandberg in his book *Nineteen Second Pole Bending*, "A horse is considered to be carrying its head in a natural position when its eyes are about level with the withers." The withers are the tops of the horse's shoulders, right where its neck starts. The reins help keep the horse's head in the right position and guide the horse as it goes along.

Ideally, the rider would use both hands on the reins for maximum maneuverability. In pole bending, the horse can skirt so close to the poles that it risks

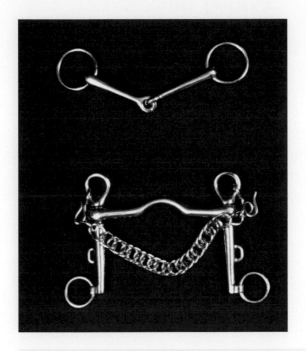

Bits like the ones pictured here *(above left)* are attached to the horse's reins and fit into its mouth *(right)*. When a rider pulls on the reins, the bit applies pressure in the horse's mouth. This pressure helps make the horse more responsive to the rider's directions and helps the rider to control the horse's speed and side-to-side motion. The twisted braid on the lower of the two bits pictured intensifies the pressure in the horse's mouth, increasing the amount of control a rider can have over her or his horse.

knocking them over, so the very experienced rider can "bend," or touch, the wobbling pole with his or her free hand as they pass, preventing the pole from toppling over. Yet one should never try to come so close to a pole, especially since righting a pole is very difficult, and usually the attempt fails.

Another important piece of tack is the bit. The bit is a metal device placed in the horse's mouth and attached to the reins. When pulled on by the reins, the bit applies pressure to various parts of the horse's mouth, making the horse responsive to a rider's desire to slow down or turn in a certain direction. Horses have a gap between their front and back teeth, and that gap is where the bit rests. There are

Cowboy Hats

Though the Stetson cowboy hat is generally made of fur felt, cowboy hats are also made out of straw. For working cowboys, the hat was a necessary and important part of the ranch wardrobe. The wide brim made quick work of fanning a campfire. The cowboy hat could also be slapped on a horse's side to give it a gentle spur. Since the hats and brims were so large, they could also be used to wave and signal to riders in the far distance.

many different kinds of bits, since different horses respond better to different kinds of pressure. Each rider will use the type that works best for him or her and the horse. A good rider will use a gentle hand with the bit and reins to avoid hurting and toughening the horse's mouth. A less sensitive mouth will make the horse less responsive on future rides.

The bit is attached to the bridle. The bridle is a system of straps, usually made of leather, that go around the horse's head, ending at the bit. The combination of the bit, bridle, and reins are what give the rider control of the direction of the horse's head, and thus the direction of the horse (generally, a horse moves in the direction its head is pointed).

PERSONAL GEAR

Generally, the only gear a rider wears is boots and a cowboy hat. Western wear is the only required gear for a pole bender. This includes cowboy boots and hat, and a long-sleeved shirt tucked into jeans. The cowboy boot dates back to at least 1870, when the high-top Wellington boot from England and V-cut Hessian military boot from Germany were combined by John Cubine in Coffeyville, Kansas, in what was called the Coffeyville-style boot.

Cowboy boots are distinctive mostly because of their decoration. While the earliest cowboy boots bore only the Lone Star of the state of Texas, the variety of

Pointed-toe cowboy boots like the ones pictured above are popular among many riders because the pointed toes help guide the foot into the stirrup. Some riders still prefer rounded-toe boots, however. The cowboy boot's high heel keeps the foot from slipping forward through the stirrup. In addition, the boot's high top protects the lower legs from jarring contact with the horse, poles, barrels, livestock, fences, or scrub vegetation. Spurs, the metal instruments that include the star-shaped rowels attached to the heels of the boots, are designed to urge on a horse, speed it up, or give directions about side-to-side movement. They help a rider communicate with it when her or his hands are busy or when it is too noisy for oral commands. A pole bender's spurs are rounded and blunted, designed to give direction without causing pain.

designs etched into the boots soon became quite varied, and now the stitching and design possibilities are seemingly infinite. Though nineteenth-century cowboys wore rounded-toe cowboy boots, the arrival of a more streamlined design in the 1940s resulted in a more pointed-toe boot. This design is now as popular as the rounded-toe among riders, and even more popular among the general public.

Carol Ellis (left foreground in red visor) conducts a pole-bending clinic at her Lazy Heart E Arena near Berthoud, Colorado, forty-five miles (seventy-two kilometers) north of Denver. Ellis conducts clinics and private lessons in pole bending, barrel racing, and beginning reining at the Lazy Heart, which is open year-round. She has been training horses for races, show competitions, and general use for more than thirty years. For pole-bending and barrel-racing horses, Ellis follows a basic step-by-step training program that focuses on first producing a solid, gentle, quiet horse, and only then introducing the horse to the poles or barrels. She believes this kind of solid training results in a horse that will both understand what its rider is asking it to do and be willing to do it.

The cowboy hat came about in 1865. It was the invention of John B. Stetson, the son of a Philadelphia hatmaker. While prospecting for gold in Colorado, Stetson grew tired of getting soaked by rain. Seeing how the coats of beavers seemed to repel water, he began to design hats made out of beaver pelts. He included a wide brim to keep rain, snow, and sun off the face and head. He also made sure to create a tall crown, where a pocket of warm air could be kept above the head, keeping it warm. This tall and waterproofed crown also allowed the hat to double as a waterbucket. This is why Stetsons are often referred to as ten-gallon hats. Stetson's hat quickly became popular among cowboys, the ultimate all-weather workers.

Small differences in hat design cropped up over the years, most of which were regional. These were often useful in identifying the geographical origin of any given cowboy, and cowboys wore their distinctive hats with pride. Now a large variety of hats exists, though the most popular brand among riders and fans alike is still Stetson.

Perhaps the most important component of a rider's personal gear is not equipment or clothing but his or her voice. As mentioned earlier, the voice is one of the four aids a rider uses to guide his or her horse during a pole-bending competition. Obviously, horses don't speak our language, but they are capable of being trained to respond to certain familiar sounds. "Whoa"(stop) is the most popular one, but others such as "walk," "back," and "trot," are just as useful. Riders and trainers must be very sure that a horse knows exactly what the commands mean. In his article "Horse Training Voice Commands," trainer Andy Curry says, "If you want your horse to slow down, then say something like 'easy.' Don't say 'slow' because he may take it for 'whoa.' Thus, when you say 'whoa' to your horse, you must only say it because you want to stop . . . not slow down."

In pole bending, voice commands, leg pressure, weight shifting, and the use of the reins must all be used in combination to get the most out of a horse. No matter how well trained the horse is, it's the communication and teamwork between a horse and rider that will win or lose a competition.

UNDERSTANDING AND COMPETING IN POLE BENDING

Pole bending is an enjoyable and exciting sport for spectators because it is very fast-paced, demonstrates the tremendous agility of horse and rider, and has very simple rules.

RULES AND PROCEDURES

Pole-bending rules and procedures are fairly rigid and consistent from competition to competition in North America. Six poles are set up in a straight line, with 21 feet (6.4 meters) separating each pole. The first pole is set up 21 feet (6.4 m) from the starting line. The poles are 6 feet (1.8 m) high, with a base that is 14 inches (35.6 centimeters) in diameter. The poles are set on top of the ground, not in holes, so the rider can "bend," or touch, them as they pass, preventing them from falling over and incurring a five-second penalty.

The horse and rider begin at a running start from well behind the start/finish line. The time clock begins when the horse's nose crosses the starting line. The horse and rider may start from either the right or left side of the poles, and the side they choose will determine which way the horse will run through the poles. In the following explanation of the layout of a pole-bending course and the horse and rider's progression through it, we will assume that they have started on the right-hand side of the poles.

After crossing the starting line, the horse runs all the way past the six poles, which are planted to its left. Upon passing the last pole, the horse turns to the left,

IGRA POLE BENDING PATTERN SET-UP

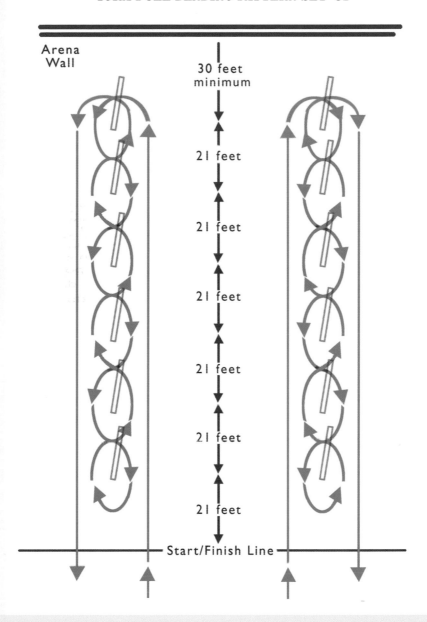

Arena
Wall

30 feet
minimum

21 feet

21 feet

21 feet

21 feet

21 feet

21 feet

Start/Finish Line

The standard arrangement of poles, the distances between them, and the pattern horse and rider must follow through a typical pole-bending course appears above. At left is the pattern a rider must follow if she or he begins with the poles on the left. At right is the pattern followed if the rider begins with the poles on her or his right.

twists around the pole, and runs diagonally between the sixth and fifth poles, keeping the fifth pole on its right. The horse then turns to the right and passes the fourth pole on its left side. Horse and rider continue this crisscrossing pattern between the poles, like a skier passing between slalom gates. When the horse weaves through all the poles, finally passing the first pole on its right side, the horse turns around the first pole and crisscrosses back through the poles, weaving in and out in the opposite direction of its first pass.

At last, the horse passes the sixth pole again, turns around it, and begins sprinting straight toward the finish line, past all the poles, which are now on the horse and rider's left-hand side. When the horse's nose crosses the line, the time clock stops.

The event is carefully timed, and the fastest time wins. However, if a pole is knocked over, a five-second penalty is added to the rider's time. In addition, if the horse does not run the course in exactly the pattern described above (whether beginning to the left or right of the poles), the team is disqualified.

ROAD TO THE TOP

Though pole-bending competitions are held weekly by many local horse and rider associations, the World Championship is governed by the American Quarter Horse Association (AQHA). The AQHA's World Championship Show is held every summer in Oklahoma City, Oklahoma. Over fourteen days, riders and horses compete in a wide variety of events, one of which is pole bending.

There are specific requirements in order to compete in the World Championship. Horses may only compete in the senior event if they have earned a total of fourteen and a half points in the monthly regional AQHA events. They may compete in a junior event if they have earned ten points. One point is awarded for every five horses that a particular horse beats in competition. So if a horse gets a better time than five other horses, it will earn one point. If a horse gets a better time than ten other horses, it will earn two points, and so on. The number of horses entered in a competition varies, since different numbers of horses show up for each event. There are also occasional double-point shows, in

Ariel C. Urban (*right*) and her mother, Debra Urban, prepare Ariel's horse, BC Sweet Hankerin, for a ride in Centerport, Pennsylvania, in June 2004. Ariel had earned a spot in the American Quarter Horse Youth Association (AQHYA) World Championship, held in July. More than 860 youths compete for world championship titles in thirty events, including pole bending, barrel racing, and various roping and jumping events.

which a horse is awarded twice the usual number of points for beating opponents, increasing the possibility for World Championship qualification.

The AQHA has two different levels based on racing experience—junior and senior. It also produces amateur competitions. Its youth division—the AQHYA—produces an annual youth World Championship as well.

For aspiring pole-bending riders, a good way to get involved is to contact a local branch of either the National FFA Organization or 4-H. The Future Farmers of America, or FFA, is an organization active in most schools and communities throughout the United States. It allows students the opportunity to experience agricultural work, including horsemanship, and, in many cases, earn class credit

Chelsi Bomar of Coryell County, Texas, expertly guides her horse through the poles during the Texas State 4-H Horse Show at the Taylor County Expo Center in Abilene, Texas, held in late July 2004.

Famous 4-H Members

Many celebrities were once members of 4-H, including Faith Hill, Johnny Carson, Dolly Parton, and Garfield creator Jim Davis, as well as former vice president Al Gore and former first lady Jacqueline Kennedy Onassis. Alan Shepard, the first American to soar beyond the earth's atmosphere into space, was also a 4-H member.

while doing so. A similar national organization, 4-H, has local chapters. The types of activities each 4-H club sponsors is determined by the local 4-H leader, so not all chapters host pole-bending competitions. However, because each branch is locally controlled, those involved in the 4-H group can often add it to the program if there is enough interest among the members.

Generally, quarter horses are used in pole bending, but many different types of horses may participate. Owning a horse is not necessary in order to compete. Some horse owners offer their horses to riders who come to them from FFA or 4-H organizations. Some racers may be put in touch with a horse owner willing to loan out or lease a horse for competition by getting jobs in horse-related workplaces, such as veterinarian's offices, stables, stockyards, and ranches.

CONCLUSION

With its mix of Eastern and Western influences and its small but dedicated community of fans and riders, pole bending is unlike any other rodeo sport. Its emphasis on speed coupled with its attention to precision horsemanship make it a truly challenging event requiring enormous skill and control from horse and rider alike. Competitors, horse owners, and fans of pole bending will likely continue to boost the popularity of this exciting rodeo event for many years to come.

For those interested in participating in pole bending, most riders and trainers interviewed for this book recommend taking basic horsemanship lessons for several years before venturing into pole bending. Horses are large and powerful animals, and the level of skill required to safely and effectively ride one through a complex obstacle course takes many years to master. And as the old adage says, a journey of 1,000 miles begins with a single step.

In *Nineteen Second Pole Bending*, trainer Wayne Sandberg puts it this way: "Any rider that will put forth the effort . . . will win their fair share of competitions. This will be a gratifying trip; you will never be sorry that you gave it your best." Whether sitting astride a horse or on arena bleachers, fans of rodeo and horsemanship will find few events as unique, entertaining, and rewarding as pole bending.

List of Champions

This table presents the American Quarter Horse Association (AQHA) World Show Results in Pole Bending, organized by year and age classification.

SENIOR/OPEN

YEAR	HORSE	RIDER
2004	Song of Badlandsskip	Kathy Ballinger
2003	Flying Humbug	Kristine Kelley
2002	Brannons Party Time	Duane Dodd
2001	Lassie Lender	George Logan
2000	Little Berseem	Clint Crider
1999	Little Berseem	Clint Crider
1998	Little Berseem	Clint Crider
1997	Little Berseem	Charles Crider
1996	Miss Querida McCue	Jamie and Jennifer Smith
1995	Rene Dan Jet	Brad Wagner
1994	Our Dirty Venture	Timothy Oxby
1993	Bambert	Janis and Patricia Wagner
1992	Lahey Lad	Gary McCoy
1991	Mr. Bar Easy	(no rider data previous to 1992)
1990	Bambert	
1989	Double Joe Win	
1988	Mr. Bar Easy	
1987	Dinky's Super Star	
1986	Precocious Sugar	
1985	Go on Gold	
1984	Moon Lights	
1983	Marshian Moon	
1982	Doc's Tex Andy	

List of Champions

YEAR	HORSE	RIDER
1981	Winners Lad	
1980	Marshian Moon	
1979	Doc Dobbin	
1978	Mr. Leo Jay	
1977	Mighty Blonde	
1976	Meers Country	
1975	Mr. Enleo	
1974	Bar the Bull	

JUNIOR/OPEN

YEAR	HORSE	RIDER
2004	Dinkys Honor Bound	Sharon Willen
2003	Doc Rancher	Elaine Elliott
2002	Magicly Rare	Jerry and Elaine Barrett
2001	Brannons Nonstop Jet	Duane Dodd
2000	Lightning Sugar Bull	David Johnting
1999	A Shadow of Thunder	Barry Joe Rich
1998	Smashed Lady Dee	Lisa Gail Gamble
1997	Regally Royally Red	Janis and Patricia Wagner
1996	Regally Royally Red	Janis Wagner
1995	Last Entry	Ross Carnahan
1994	Flying Humbug	Ross Carnahan
1993	Cooks Sugar King	David Johnting
1992	Brays Dancing Lark	Dennis Hildebrand
1991	The Flying Bug	(no rider data previous to 1992)
1990	Maybe Doctor Jay	

List of Champions

YEAR	HORSE	RIDER
1989	Mr. Rock a Doc	
1988	Lofty Dew Bars	
1987	Kims Chip	
1986	Dinky's Super Star	
1985	Mr. Bar Easy	
1984	Mr. Bar Easy	
1983	Moon Lights	
1982	Moon Lights	
1981	One by One Time	
1980	Leo Rastus Charge	
1979	Wilda Chapo	
1978	Winners Lad	
1977	Mr. Triple Sandy	
1976	(no data for this year)	
1975	Brother Luke	
1974	High Bars Wimpy	

YOUTH

YEAR	HORSE	RIDER
2004	Bayou a Trip	Kelli Johnson
2003	Moonette Miss	Veronica Handegan
2002	Prices Penny Ace	Preston Collins
2001	Mr. Little Brown Jug	Tisha Linn Burress
2000	Mr. Little Brown Jug	Tisha Linn Burress
1999	The Flying Bug	Amy McClung

List of Champions

YEAR	HORSE	RIDER
1998	Invisible Touch	Kassidy Danyel Jones
1997	Little Berseem	Clint Crider
1996	Mr. Bar Easy	Chad Crider
1995	Miss Querida McCue	Jennifer Driver
1994	Cleo Grinder	Rachael Christenson
1993	Miss Querida McCue	Jennifer Driver
1992	Smoky 2	Troy Priddy
1991	Cactus Cabana	Rebecca Baker
1990	Miss Querida McCue	Jamie Smith
1989	Rovin Revenge	Angela Mullins
1988	Speckled Now	Shannon Williams
1987	Go on Gold	Rob Hall
1986	Lightasafeather	Camy Enlow
1985	Black Enuf	Cary Quakenbush
1984	Baldy Boy Leo	Tammy Chilton
1983	Big Ben Jr.	Robbie Stacy
1982	Flashy's Baby	Dean Monk
1981	Third Dancer	Tammy Crowder
1980	Keep Fiddlin	Joanne Hamill
1979	Crooked Harry	Kristin Rathert
1978	Foolish Bar	Elizabeth Hildebrandt
1977	Rob's Troublemaker	Myra Riddle
1976	Miss Heidi 2	Michelle Miller
1975	Dangerous Spark	Andrea Fischer
1974	Four Corners Boy	Bobby Dearing
1973	Dear Bar's Baby	Robin Powell
1972	Mr. Belvedere	Tammy Strack

List of Champions

AMATEUR

YEAR	HORSE	RIDER
2004	Dinkys Honor Bound	Lonnie Willen
2003	Song of Badlandsskip	Kathy Ballinger
2002	Speedy Prissy Doc	Wenda Johnson
2001	Lassie Lender	Darrell Logan
2000	Iam a Venterized Man	Kyle Campbell
1999	Iam a Venterized Man	Kyle Campbell
1998	Myers Easy Does It	Kirby Milem
1997	A Sharp Nesian	Brannon Riley
1996	Rene Dan Jet	Brad Wagner
1995	Miss Querida McCue	Jamie Smith
1994	Bambert	Janis Wagner
1993	The Flying Bug	Stephanie Essman
1992	Bambert	Janis Wagner
1991	Lahey Lad	Gary McCoy
1990	Pretty Boy Buzz	Jenell Kern
1989	Pretty Boy Buzz	Jenell Kern
1988	Precocious Sugar	Dianne Marie Kenney
1987	Precocious Sugar	Dianne Marie Kenney
1986	Go on Gold	Judy Wadino
1985	Bruces Bright Bar	Helene Dickinson
1984	Marshian Moon	Kim Letterman
1983	Maco Bar	Laurie Gray
1982	Misty Lady Jane	Steven Benefiel
1981	Skeeter's Best	Rosemary Johns
1980	Smoky 2	Layman Priddy

Glossary

bit The metal mouthpiece of a bridle that serves to control, curb, and direct an animal.

bridle Gear including a headstall, bit, and reins, fitted about a horse's head and used to restrain or guide the animal.

dressage The guiding of a horse through a series of complex maneuvers controlled and directed through slight movements of the rider's hands, legs, and weight.

gymkhana A meet at which riders and horses display a range of horsemanship skills.

mare A female horse or the female of other equine species.

reins A long, narrow leather strap attached to each end of the bit of a bridle and used by a rider or driver to control a horse or other animal.

rodeo A public competition or exhibition in which skills such as riding broncos or roping calves are displayed.

saddle A seat for the rider of a horse.

saddle horn A high knobby portion of a Western saddle (usually metal, covered with leather).

stirrup A flat-based loop or ring hung from either side of a horse's saddle to support the rider's foot in mounting and riding.

tack The harness for a horse, including the bridle and saddle.

vaquero Local name of Spanish origin for a cowboy (vaquero is used especially in southwestern and central Texas, while buckaroo is used especially in California).

withers The high part of the back of a horse or similar animal, located between the shoulder blades.

For More Information

The American Quarter Horse Association
P.O. Box 200
Amarillo, TX 79168
(806) 376-4811
Web site: http://www.aqha.com

National Little Britches Rodeo Association
1045 W. Rio Grande
Colorado Springs, CO 80906
(800) 763-3694
Web site: http://www.nlbra.com

Northwest Youth Rodeo Association
973 Dearborn Avenue
N. Keizer, OR 97303
Web site: http://www.nwyra.com

Southwestern Pole Bending Association
6060 Linne Road
Paso Robles, CA 93446
(805) 238-9818
Web site: http://www.pole-bending.com

WEB SITES

Due to the changing nature of Internet links, the Rosen Publishing Group, Inc., has developed an online list of Web sites related to the subject of this book. This site is updated regularly. Please use this link to access the list:

http://www.rosenlinks.com/woro/pobe

For Further Reading

Alter, Judy. *Rodeos: The Greatest Show on Dirt.* New York, NY: Franklin Watts, 1996.

Campion, Lynn. *Rodeo: Behind the Scenes at America's Most Exciting Sport.* Guilford, CT: The Lyons Press, 2002.

Crum, Robert. *Let's Rodeo!: Young Buckaroos and the World's Wildest Sport.* New York, NY: Simon & Schuster Children's Publishing, 1996.

Fredriksson, Kristine. *American Rodeo: From Buffalo Bill to Big Business.* College Station, TX: Texas A&M Press, 1993.

Lecompte, Mary Lou. *Cowgirls of the Rodeo: Pioneer Professional Athletes.* Champaign, IL: University of Illinois Press, 2000.

Stratton, W. K. *Chasing the Rodeo: On Wild Rides and Big Dreams, Broken Hearts and Broken Bones, and One Man's Search for the West.* New York, NY: Harcourt, 2005.

Bibliography

Alabama Open Horseman Association. "2005 State Show Rules." Retrieved May 2005 (http://www.showaoha.org/rules.htm).

Ballinger, Kathy, in discussion with the author, April 2005.

Beard, Tyler. "The Art of the Boot." *Texas Monthly*. Retrieved May 2005 (http://www.texasmonthly.com/mag/issues/hot/2000-01-01/artoftheboot.html).

Chavez, Donald Gilbert Y. "Cowboys—Vaqueros: Origins of the First American Cowboys." University of New Mexico. Retrieved May 2005 (http://www.unm.edu/~gabbriel/index.html).

Curry, Andy. "Horse Training Voice Commands." HorseTrainingAndTips.com. 2004. Retrieved May 2005 (http://www.horsetrainingandtips.com/horse_training_commands.htm).

Draper, Judith, Debbie Sly, and Sarah Muir. *Complete Book of Horses and Riding*. New York, NY: Barnes & Noble Books, 2003.

Dressage World. "History of Dressage." Retrieved May 2005 (http://www.worlddressage.com/history.htm).

Hamilton, Christine. "Amateur Pole Bending Finals: This Horse Does It on His Own." American Quarter Horse Association. 2004. Retrieved May 2005 (http://www.aqha.com/showing/shows/worldshow/winningrun/amateurpolebending.html).

Hollister, Kyla. "Senior Pole Bending Finals: Kathy Ballinger and Song of Badlandsskip Win Back-to-Back World Titles." American Quarter Horse Association. 2004. Retrieved May 2005 (http://www.aqha.com/showing/shows/worldshow/winningrun/seniorpolebendingfinals.html).

Michigan Horse Council. "U.S. Tent Pegging Assn., Jeff Kalman." 2005. Retrieved May 2005 (http://www.michiganhorsecouncil.com/expo/2005expo/demos/tent.htm).

Quaid, Ronda. "A Tip of the Hat to the Vaqueros." Coastline. 1996. Retrieved May 2005 (http://www.silcom.com/~imago/sbnp/rodeohist.html).

The Saddle Zone. "The Evolution of the Western Saddle." 2002. Retrieved May 2005 (http://saddlezone.com/html-top/saddle_history.htm).

Pole Bending

Sandberg, Wayne. *Nineteen Second Pole Bending*. Calgary, Canada: Dakota Design and Advertising, 2005.

Smith, Ken. "Pole Bending Horsemanship Principles for Success at Pole Bending and Barrel Racing." Sunrise West Quarter Horses. 2005. Retrieved May 2005 (http://www.sunrisewest.com/help.html).

Wooden, Wayne S., and Gavin Ehringer. *Rodeo in America: Wranglers, Roughstock, and Paydirt*. Lawrence, KS: University Press of Kansas, 1996.

Index

Pole Bending

ABOUT THE AUTHOR

Matthew Broyles is originally from Texas, where his family has been involved in ranch work for at least a century. One of his first jobs was working with horses at a veterinarian's office, and he grew up attending rodeos. He currently resides in Brooklyn, New York, and has written one other book for Rosen.

PHOTO CREDITS

Designer: Les Kanturek